Bones Washed With Wine

Flint Shards from Sussex and *Bliss*

Award-Winning Poetry Collection

Jeff Mann

Arlington, Virginia

BONES WASHED WITH WINE: FLINT SHARDS FROM SUSSEX and BLISS.
Copyright © 2003 by Jeff Mann.
FLINT SHARDS FROM SUSSEX Copyright © 1999 by Jeff Mann, published by
Gival Press, LLC.
BLISS Copyright © 1998 by Jeff Mann, published by BrickHouse Books.

All rights reserved under International and Pan-American Copyright Conventions.
Printed in the United States of America.

With the exception of brief quotations in the body of critical articles or reviews, no part of this book may be reproduced or transmitted in any form or by any means, graphic, electronic, or mechanical, including photocopying, recording, taping, or by any information storage or retrieval system, without the permission in writing from the publisher.

Published by Gival Press, an imprint of Gival Press, LLC.
For information please write:
Gival Press, LLC, P. O. Box 3812, Arlington, VA 22203.
Website: www.givalpress.com

First Edition ISBN 1-928589-14-6
Library of Congress Control Number: 2002108616

Photo of Jeff Mann by John Ross.
Format and design by Ken Schellenberg.

Acknowledgments

"Pupae" was published in *Christopher Street*.
"Scotch and Valentines" was published in *Dead Snakes, Cats, and the IRS: Poetry of Rock and Rebellion*, edited by Anne Cheney.
"Moss Rose" was published in *Kinesis*.
"Biscuits and Honey" was published in *Amethyst*.
"Leaf Stains" was published in *The Hampden-Sydney Poetry Review*.
"Another Droning Dismissal" was published in *Kestrel*.
"The Crowbar Comes" was published in *Yemassee*.
"Duckpond in October" was published in *Nexus*.
"Bliss" was published in *BlackWater Review*.
"Not Getting Off at Farragut North" was published in *The Spoon River Poetry Review*.

Praise for Jeff Mann's Work

"...[A] book of lyric intensity, focusing on love through the radiance of martyrdom and sacrifice. In the poet's journey away from America to the land of *Wuthering Heights*, he immerses himself in the dark beauty of romantic loss, grieving, and final acceptance."

—Diane Wakoski, author of *Argonaut Rose*

"Jeff Mann writes poetry as specific as a 'reliquary's budding rubies,' as sensual as 'the scent / of smoke, the feel of phlox,' as rich as 'laburnum flowers, liquid gold.' He is a poet to treasure both for the wealth of his language and the generosity of his spirit."

—Edward Falco, author of *Acid*

"... a moving lyric sequence of love poems. Love lost. As mile by mile, and poem by poem, the speaker seeks to distance himself from loss, the pages refill with the spectral, as though the ocean were foaming into empty footprints. A travel itinerary of vivid English landscapes provides sparkling scenes but no solace. Rather, journey becomes only the space where 'peace is nothing but convalescence...fuel for the next flowering.' The pulse of these poems rests not only in personal toll but also in greater losses informed by history, literature and the land itself. Mann creates a sensuous feast of the English countryside, and of the human body. In prismatic flashes, that which is absent returns, 'as if sunlight had a weight...this is how you descend / again, this congregation of gold.' A poignant collection."

—Katherine Soniat, author of *A Shared Life*

"These fiercely lyrical poems ignite us and make us remember what it means to 'experience' a poem as we read it."

—Jan-Mitchell Sherrill

"A sophisticated collection of provocative verse, Jeff Mann's poems themselves 'torch our throats,' but more than twice or thrice."

—K. Edgington, Towson University

Also by Jeff Mann

Mountain Fireflies

Edge

For my family
and the many friends
who've helped me survive
my own intensity

Contents

Flint Shards From Sussex

Gold Dust	12
Departure	13
Time Zones	15
Patcham Churchyard	17
Azaleas, Leeds Castle	19
Icons	21
Elgin Marbles	22
Preston Manor Gardens	25
Laburnum	27
Gray Lady	29
Wax	33
Insatiate	34
Yearning	35
Whirlpool	36
Devil's Dyke	37

Bliss

Moss Rose	41
The Crowbar Comes	42
Risk	43
Pupae	45
Bliss	48
Buchenwald	51
New Market Battlefield	53
March Magnolias	55
Three Lovers At Walden Pond	57
Duck Pond In October	60
Bones Washed With Wine	62
Peepers	64
Biscuits And Honey	66
Confederate Cemetery, Fredericksburg, Virginia	68
Scotch And Valentines	70
Another Droning Dismissal	72
Not Getting Off At Farragut North	74
Leaf Stains	76

Flint Shards from Sussex

That, however, which you may suppose the most potent to arrest my imagination, is actually the least, for what is not connected with her to me? and what does not recall her? I cannot look down to this floor, but her features are shaped on the flags! In every cloud, in every tree—filling the air at night, and caught by glimpses in every object by day, I am surrounded with her image! The most ordinary faces of men and women—my own features—mock me with a resemblance. The entire world is a dreadful collection of memoranda that she did exist, and that I have lost her!

—Emily Brontë, *Wuthering Heights*

Gold Dust

This is the danger:
locating meaning
in another face, body,

life. As if meaning were
a trace element,
a specific density,

gold dust almost
always elsewhere,
rare as

pieces of
the True Cross,
a vial of God's blood

locked behind
the reliquary's
budding rubies.

Then breath is
always leaving
ice trails, smoke trails.

Flesh is the hollow
sycamore within which
a solitary huddles

and starves, the tossed
shell a hermit crab borrows
for want of a better home.

Departure

Leaving for England this afternoon,
clutching my redneck cap against the wind.

Driving from D.C. to Dulles Airport,
speeding out of adultery and America,

too fast past your exit—Falls Church, Sycamore Street—
that road ramping straight into rapture

reserved for another.
Are you napping this afternoon,

or sipping a beer on your balcony, amidst
the catmint, the dittany of Crete?

We are cunning. We leave no clues.
Hot showers, my inventoried packing,

sandalwood incense exorcizing
the smell of sex. On your surface, I leave

no bruises, no trace. No evidence but this paper
trail, the cursive of mountain backroads,

the flatlines of interstates
leading away from how well

the silver earring I bought you
complements your lapis wedding ring.

Those brief and furtive weekends,
your lover out of town,

I stroked your chest hair like young grass,
aspen's new leaves. Tenderness

made me an artesian well, and the banks
of ghostly white azaleas some firebomb

beneath my breastbone answered. What lack
of mine insures this absence?

To drive hurriedly by a street
where bliss waits for luckier men,

to turn away from what one most loves.
What banal necessity. Even the comet

has no choice in its great parabola. It sweeps
as close to the sun as its orbit allows,

then turns away
and is sucked back into darkness,

trailed by its own imperfect burning.

Time Zones

On the plane I wanted to murder
a baby. Instead, I sipped two Drambuies—free!—

I worked in earplugs, those daffodil slugs,
I stared at Brad Pitt's lips. I do not possess

the technology needed to gauge
the exact distance between your bed

in Falls Church, Virginia, and this spot
on Heathrow's tarmac, my first English step.

A bunch of yellow roses on the breakfast table,
one for each day I stayed. As they withered,

as we argued, you neatly picked them out
and trashed them. A neat difference between us:

I would have made potpourri.
Now geography coincides with fact—

we are all the Atlantic apart. Dumb with jet lag,
I unpack, sip tea, nuzzle lilacs

and wish they had your scent.
You sleep still, five hours behind—is your husband

home yet? The sheets leave creases on your sides,
your back shaved for the beach beginning

to fur over again, fern garden I love.
Marriage must be

the small gestures
I have always missed—shaving

a lover's back, buying him deodorant,
a new computer game, complaining about

his rank socks in August. "If
I'd met you first. . ." If Harold

had not fallen at Hastings. Our timing
was always off. It has denied me

a language, a life.

Patcham Churchyard

From the packed bone meal
of these generations,
all that passion

like mine
so long composted,
from the South Downs chalk,

the cemetery lilacs spring.
I bend bunches down,
for long minutes

press my beard deep and sigh.
A pigeon calls. I might have begged,
but you gave with little asking,

bending back on the couch, slipping
your legs over my shoulders,
groaning softly as I moved

inside you, May easing sepals open.
Our moustaches melted,
still sticky with honey,

that insufficient glue,
its sweetness
surpassed,

surpassed, surpassed.
Your breath was my air,
my ecstasy, arriving together.

There is the stillness of churchyards,
and this: easing out of you,
where the axes of the cross,

the axes of the Milky Way meet,
the hurricane has its core,
my face buried

in your chest hair,
your heart beating against my brow—
the rhythm of waves along Brighton's

beach, the bedside clock, the train
moving across the mountainside.
Curled in my childhood bunk bed

I hear it, the pulse that makes night
amniotic. We can list them, the few
seconds we would die into.

We would give up all else.
We would listen to that heartbeat
forever, not rise from the bed

which is only lifting my face
from a bunch of English lilacs
and moving on, heading down the hill to tea.

Azaleas, Leeds Castle

Beyond the carved ceiling beams,
the moated castle walls, beyond the drift
of blood-beaked black swans,

banks and banks of flame azalea.
The voice of the burning bush,
the bonfire, says always,

"Enter."
What little interest
I have always had in leaves,

roots, fruit, bark. What little interest
in serenity. It is a compulsion,
burying my face in petals

as if I would eat them,
their founts, their hemorrhage.
As if I would inhale fire.

I break my own bones in half
like brittle kindling
in order to feed such a flame,

willing to sacrifice anything.
To bloom not once a year,
the weak muster of vegetation,

but as often as the body can bear.
So each ecstasy is brief?
Then let it come more often.

Till another life teach

the mystery of fruit and harvest,
peace is nothing

but convalescence,
a slow gathering of twigs and bark,
fuel for the next flowering, the next fire.

Icons

What the exile most longs for—
someone to speak to, even
in absence, the azure
of aerogrammes, the fogged

windows of buses one fingers
these rainy nights,
the sand one cuts initials into
with a tide-smoothed stone.

Prayer must have some direction,
some compass point towards which
we aim our eyes, our folded hands,

our sighs. Entering the chapel,
look for icons. Someone to intercede.
Before the statues, the suffering
stretched out in metal, stone or wood,

the candles are banked, the flowers heaped.
God's knees or feet are rubbed
to a shimmer, are begged to burnished gold.

Elgin Marbles

Different continent, same obsessions.
Fixation is a boomerang,

and the world's reduced
to memoranda, Heathcliff said.

Very little I notice does not
lead back to you,

lover, ant lion, pinpoint gateway
at the whirlpool's base,

blood draining from a puncture wound,
water sucking from the tub,

leaving the body propped and cold.
In the British Museum, what moves me,

as it did that waning boy from Hampstead,
is incompletion

which was once complete:
the Elgin marbles,

the bog-browned corpse
of the Lindow Man.

Faces smudged, limbs
chipped or gone entirely.

We surmise the story
in shards, like

a life written
in that fickle ink

that smears to a blue wash
in the rain.

Among the statuary, your chest
and flanks are everywhere,

in pieces I would nuzzle,
were I bolder, madder,

my mouth
moistening marble

to a glisten. Not that
longing before the kiss,

where Keats would freeze it. Instead,
the way our muscles strain together.

I would make marble of us
then, just this side of exhaustion,

though even our aftermath is art,
your heart slowing against my temple,

your dark chest hair
stippling with silver.

The Lindow Man was handsome
and bearded once like you, before

the stone to the head, the garrote,
the blade, the staining centuries

of the bog seep, curled in the earth
as you curl against me in sleep.

Only fire will spare us that shriveling,
or, more mundane, that liquefaction

on satin. Till then,
before all we knew came to ruin,

I was a witness.
I touched

a magnitude,
not the shadow of a magnitude.

Before flesh fell to fragments,
I loved your beauty whole.

Preston Manor Gardens

(for Annette Oxindine)

From the bus's top deck I've glimpsed it
many times, a garden sheltered behind

high flint walls over which the lilacs
foam, inaccessible as some island

riding the horizon, as the Milky Way,
there to remind us of all those riches

reserved for others, all we cannot touch.
So I am surprised this sunny day,

deciding to work off ales and walk
for once, to find this small ivy-edged door.

Open. Entering, I feel furtive,
wandering along the flowering

laburnum avenues, bending down
to champagne and indigo irises,

stretching up to clematis,
bunch after bunch of lilacs, purple and white.

A tiny sign says "Breath of Life."
We kissed first four years ago,

in my office. Your cheek was rough,
your moustache tickled my lips.

Rapture is so seldom.
I'd thought it walled off

long ago. Today, as then, I am
guilty, tentative, apologetic,

expecting the flaming sword,
as if denial were something

deserved. The concept of grace
assumes we are all unworthy.

I have seen the serpent
in the mirror,

I expect exile any minute,
for ecstasy is something one must steal.

Meanwhile
petals and stamens

tickle my eager face like fur,
my beard is dusted with gold,

with humility.
Who ever would have guessed,

whisper the blessed,
such a garden

would ever have opened its gates
to me?

Laburnum

Every time you peel off your shirt,
then mine, bend over me,
lower yourself slowly into kisses,

as if sunlight had a weight,
muscles stretched out along my length,
I speak to you, then more than you, saying,

> So this is how you descend
> again, this congregation of gold,
>
> coins and rings showering my torso's
> thick grass, scalding the coverlet
>
> of my brow, embers swarming
> the age-cracked concrete.
>
> Combustible wings and keels,
> tiny ships wherein the body ascends,
>
> smoke along a sea wind.
> Beneath the laburnum tree,
>
> I stretch out my arms.
> Nail me here,
>
> nail me to this light,
> your body's petal-drift upon mine.
>
> Make flame
> of my flesh.

I am strong enough.
Leave nothing unconsumed.

Let every impure atom's ash
ride off on wind. What is left

of us, pooling together—
laburnum flowers, liquid gold.

Gray Lady

The hawthorns are wounded here
near the end of Meeting House Lane.

At dusk a sea breeze shivers down
these stained pink petals, incriminating

scrim through which she steps,
a gray-cowled nun. In death

she has lost her face—
a slate smear as of cloud banks

deluging the distant downs,
pencil lead shaded in and rubbed hard beneath

a frantic thumb. He was too beautiful,
that soldier striding the narrow lanes

of medieval Brighton. By late afternoon
stubble shaded his jaw like black sand.

In the cloister alone at night she heard the sea,
in dream she ran her hands through that sand,

along the edge of his sword. At last prayers
had purpose. What ruse did she use to escape

that first night, to meet him in the hawthorn grove?
The pink petals, falling, flecked them both

with dilute blood. He wanted her as well—
the miracle for which she was willing to pay.

He locked the door, he snuffed the candle.
He smelt like smoke. Rain rilled its descent,

erratic down the diamond-leaded glass.
Eager as surf, she foamed

her fingers along his jaw,
through the hair on his chest

and back, phlox mats
in the convent garden she had stroked

for years. She had a body now,
and all could tell. Tasting that,

how could she renounce him, how return
to the life she had known? I want to believe that,

saving her once, he tried to save her
again. I want to believe the miracle had been mutual,

that he had to be dragged from the execution
in chains—though, being a soldier, he was spared

her fate. Breaking the vows of chastity:
she was bricked up alive.

She did not struggle,
walled in already

by the flesh he had given her,
the longing she had found

every time they parted.
In this final cloister areek with mortar,

the memory of his flesh—the scent
of smoke, the feel of phlox—

was not enough
bread, water, air.

Her breath ran out
as this pen empties of ink.

He was freed too late, his fists'
blood disappearing, disguised by brick.

Why does she walk?
She was but newly awake—

in the weight of his body,
dawn first entered her.

She was not ready to sleep again so soon.
He was too beautiful, the earth

too beautiful to leave so easily,
so early. The doom of any great desire—

like the shingle a gray nun once loved to hear
rattling over itself on broken waves retreating.

Like the waves themselves.
How weary they must be,

caught sleepless between the shore and sea,
never to rest, always to seek,

stroking and clawing
the receding lover, the eroding coast.

Wax

Each lights the other's candle,
rubs the shaft with oils—

musk, patchouli—or heather honey.
Flame turns the wax transparent.

Each drips the burning
in the other's chest hair.

I want to see you wince
as I smear my name, my epitaph,

across your nipples in flame,
then lower myself upon you

till the wax hardens between us,
a few seconds seal us together.

INSATIATE

Night rain clinging to the panes
winks gold against black
in the street lamp light.

Those seconds between
the heart's stoppage
and the brain's

are all hunger.
Your hand in my hands,
I feel your knucklebones.

For touch,
there is never time enough.
Look around: every goodbye

might be the last.
It is the only way
to die, wanting more.

Yearning

Stand in any pub corner
and watch. For so few,
so few are allotted

these barside hugs, fingers
run along a denimed thigh,

the guarantee of nightfall,
a kiss become a promise.

The rest of us will settle,
because we must, for

too many beers, a hot plate
of fish and chips, rice pudding,

or the wicked sublimation
of spotted dick.

To yearn so deeply,
so far from the object

of that longing,
is to leave your life,

your bloodbeat, your breath,
always to be where
and when you are not.

Whirlpool

In these Rottingdean gardens
once owned by Kipling,

there grows,
according to the guide,

the world's most fragrant rose
clambering up this wall of knapped flint.

Tourists line up to sniff. I wait
till I'm alone, then after nuzzling

the bloom, I slip in a finger, then
a tongue, then take a bite of petal.

Like standing in a red shaft
of stained-glass light,

the vortex of a vampire's thirst.
The beloved's body

is a whirlpool,
any opening that leads inside,

beyond. The rose spreads slowly,
the horizons swirl around me,

and I slip wholly into
bloodbeat, into darkness.

Devil's Dyke

All your life you have belonged only here,
listening to wind, to leaves, feeling

the chill deepen on this height about
Devil's Dyke, in this rough wind rushing

dusk down upon you, rustling trees
about the pub. You could step inside,

but there is no one here to speak truth to
above the fried fish and pints of bitter beer.

Better to stand apart, in silence
save for this sky's hiss over the downs,

distant students' hacky-sack laughter.
Ingrate—all these treasures of hedgerow,

pasture and hill spilled out before you, yet
you insist only on beauty that might return

your touch. You would choose,
like any heretic. Now eyesight fails

with evening, the downs disappear.
From this edge of green turned gray,

you turn back, along the chalk path
still easy to follow, like a sun-bleached

spine. Far above, the swallows veer,
vectors too free and erratic to follow.

They fly in pairs.
You will die far from your kind.

BLISS

Moss Rose

Secular as pig's purslaine, as our daily bread,
its leaves are kneaded from ash, from sand,

retaining water as desert plants do. By mid-morning,
like succulents after a storm, the blossoms

are scalding the porch, a ravelling of pentagrams,
cups full of fireworks, gullets spilling with

dwarf stars. These are the flowers that torch
our throats only twice or thrice a lifetime, leaving

our spines like abandoned wicks. Most of our breaths,
mere fallow between flames. Like lightning rods,

we wait for accidents, for magma to run along
our muscles, our marrow to fill with sparks.

Like the moss rose, we choke with joy on
our own flammability, for some face to split us open

with unmitigated morning, some face to lend us fire.

The Crowbar Comes

(for Dark Shadows *fans)*

Long, long, I have slept like a grub,
curled within a chrysalis of satin
glass, crabbed in this chained
coffin behind a sealed mausoleum
door. A century of afternoons
I have drowsed the way reptiles
slow in cold, the way vipers
dream of the heat their pits will
thrum towards. I see his neck:
beneath a day's stubble-grit,
the great artery, iambic, throbs.
On my own teeth I cut my tongue.
The dusk stretches its jaws,
swallows the hot sun whole.
All night I strain against ebony,
a sky without a star. The links
rattle and curse. My father put me
here. It may take centuries more,
but one will come. My tongue tastes
his heartbeat, the hiss of his breath,
across continents, across autumns.
Hunger or greed or curiosity
will lift the crowbar, my palms
will unclench. God help
the man who breaks the lock,
who shoulders the boulder aside,
who in my ceiling's unchained
rending, lets slip his eyes
I seize like fireflies, like falling stars.

RISK

Dinner over, we walk off mint juleps,
down a path busy with bikers and joggers,
the tremble of lovesick aspen, honeysuckle
banks, elderberry froth I bend to your nose.
Driving as wildly into ripeness as we,
these cornfields, the distant horizon
of Brush Mountain. I notice the first
tiny lines across your brow as you grin
at a joke and soft-punch my arm,
I try to memorize the colors in
your frank and fond high-summer eyes.

In twilight's first hint, with what tenderness
do you catch a passing firefly on your fingertip.
"Good omens," you say, as the mourning dove
yearns above bulrushes, as the red-winged
blackbird, all intensity of poppy-fire
and poppy-black, leaps off a wire, as
a tiny insect creeps from its chrysalis
and clings dizzy with rebirth along an aster stem.

> Whenever you enter my sight, my arms,
> summer saturates us, evolution accelerates,
> nakedness rilling with honey and sunlight.
> No sense of mine, made modest by loneliness,
> ever dreamed such surpassing. Only you ever
> made my love welcome, could face half my fire.

Leaving the busier paths behind—
sad adolescents with Walkman withdrawal,
old couples trailing leashed dogs—we walk
above the cornfields and into woods:
Appalachian summer shade of white oaks,
sweet cicely, jewelweed, Hester Prynne's escape.
Only in the forest do we touch.

Alone at last, I reach for you. You pull back,
peering fearfully about brief vistas
of only trunk and leaf. What letters
would madmen carve on our chests?
About your shorter but twice-as-strong frame
I wrap an arm, imagining with what bear-fury
I would knife any threat to you, some attacker's
blood splashing over my shuddering hands.

And so we walk, naming the species of trees
and shrubs, pointing out the pale trail
of lightning along a dead oak, hearing in distance
wasp-drone interstate traffic. Ears and eyes
always wary, ready to fly apart like atoms.
This tenderness could kill us. Nevertheless
at forest-edge I turn, bend down to honeysuckle
alchemies of moustache and lips. At risk,
your handsome face, your restless brain.
So easily shattered. Sudden fists, knives,
and all your hard-muscled health's unknit,
irreparable in a second, chrysalis crushed,
a heap of sticky crystal. Our hands part

as we leave the woods, as the sun puddles
into purple over Brush Mountain, as
I recall the heckles, recall the swell
of a punched lip, a friend's bones found
in the town dump, beyond any peril or safety.

Pupae

Mortimer Junior: Why should you love him whom the world hates so?

Edward: Because he loves me more than all the world:
    Ah, none but rude and savage-minded men
    Would seek the ruin of my Gaveston...

—Christopher Marlowe, *Edward the Second*

1

Beneath us the earthworms in
their darkness are content.
The grubs curl tight
and dream of wings.
Encamped under stone,
niched within wood,
cemented in chrysalids,
the sowbug, the termite,
the monarch.
In October's cellar,
the coal-dust cricket
chirps. Holes befit only
the half-formed, the minuscule.

2

Gaveston of Gascony, eldritch
and green-eyed, black curls
as soft as larch feathering
across his breastbone—savages
"in a trench / Strake off his head."
King Edward peasants took with a poker
still smoking from the coals.
I hear their love words, their
shrieks, as I grip your hand.

All the long drive up the Shenandoah,
you feed me bits of blueberry scone as I steer,
you bite my bare shoulder, stroke my beard,
to the wide-eyed strain of passing faces,
the shock and hate and hoot. Our defiant
political delight is permitted only by
the safety of speeding at 65. In the garden
of the National Cathedral, among the frowsy
fragrance of roses, lavender beds, featherings
of dill, I want to hold you hard despite
the heat, but this garden is earthly,
with riven walls. Fear slithers in.

In an empty hall of the great tower's
observation deck, we peer both ways—
criminals, children crossing the street—
then hurriedly kiss. Only with evening,
in air-conditioned privacy, behind a series
of locks, the opaque permission of plaster walls,
only then do I nudge my head into your lap,
only then you smooth my thinning hair.

Habits linger. Hitting Dupont Circle bars
after dinner, we sip Molsons for five minutes
before you turn on your stool grinning, "I forgot.
I can touch you here," and pat the empty wedge of seat
between your legs. So I sit, your stubble-dark cheek
against my neck, your hairy hard arms about my chest,
a torch song whispered in my ears. My friends tease us,
I bare my fangs at them and smilingly soak up
all the affections my adolescence missed.

Long before the bar door we separate. Somewhere,
a gay teenager nurses his split lip,
a lesbian not yet sixteen closes the garage
door and turns the car key. On some nearby street,
Edward is screaming yet, Gaveston's head rolls
like roadside litter, as I shoulder us out onto P Street,

craning for bashers and bristling like a wolf, knowing
how easily your skin would split and scar,
how simply your breath could stop.
How many lifetimes will always lack this tenderness
welling in me as I watch you stride cautiously up
the sidewalk, as you step towelling down from the shower,
as you grin drowsily in our sticky unroped aftermath,
as your sleeping face forms beside me in the dawn.
Amidst rude and savage-minded men,
what is more dangerous than tenderness?

3

Loving the endangered, loving the fragile:
these needful follies most make us political.
The insect's dark pupae—soon these will be past,
so small the spaces where love is safe,
the closet molds, the cellar suffocations,
all in the difference of a door.
Love comes too seldom to be secret,
to choke like a crocus beneath concrete.
Too ancient, too great a power welds our hands.
Look around: we are too many, too strong,
too fine for holes. See how brave the young become.
Breathe deeply: the air and the light are ours.

Bliss

Leaving State College, Pennsylvania.
Proud gourmet, I prove my love by agreeing
to fast food. Drive-through chicken nuggets
and fries you sweeten with barbeque sauce
and feed me while I drive, affections
that elicit the occasional craning
and sanctimony of passing strangers.

Nearly a week together careful deceit
has allowed us: the laugh and shove
of sheet-top wrestlers, Canadian beer,
amalgam scents of semen and leather and sweat,
your untouchable moods, your critical tongue,
my lion's brooding pout. Making love
without our wristwatches, sleeping at last
all naked night, side by side, a luxury
for adulterers. One week. Now
I am driving us back home.

Nuggets over, the exhaustions of conference
and job interviews catch up with you.
Your chin bounces on your chest a bit,
a mile or two, then uncoaxed you settle
your head onto my lap and into deep sleep.

This landscape I hardly see—dry with July,
humid-hazy hills, the rocky low stretch
of the Susquehanna. Instead I am cursing
each noisy truck that ruckuses by, every
shock-shaking pavement bump. You sleep
through it all, legs folded up like a child's,
lying on your side on the short truck seat,
cheek soft pressure of bliss on my thigh.

You sleep through Pennsylvania's remainder,
Maryland, West Virginia, and into Virginia.
My leg numbs, will shift for nothing,
is finally forgotten. My right arm I arch
awkward over your face to shade your eyes.
Your breath is hot on my hand.

How many idylls is any life allotted?
On and off for hours I look down on
dark eyebrows, a cheek shaved this morning
already stubble-shaded, a few gray hairs
on your temples, that restless mind at rest,
all your bitchery, your critical scalpels,
sunk beneath this smooth lapped vulnerability.
You who refuse to sleep close, to be held
in morning's first moments, today you leave
your life to me, trusted to my steerage.

I want to take a new exit, make this week's escape
permanent, drive with you through dawn
after dawn, dusk after dusk, through towns full
of maples and turrets and morning glories,
towns where we would not be found:
a fantasy farmhouse isled in elms,
flower beds you landscape long, a table
heavy with biscuits and shoo-fly pie,
a bed we could share for decades, bear-paw quilts,
four strong posts to withstand your struggle.

Watching you sleep, my love is all honest,
unselfconscious, no need to hold back or hide.
I adjust my arm against the sun, you shift
without waking onto your back, small bare
feet propped against the window glass.
How few the seconds of our lives we would stall
into perpetuity, how rare the welling of joy
in the throat. With every touch you teach me
how pale was any day before I ever called happy.

So we enter with evening the Shenandoah Valley,
the moon comes clear and you wake,
four hours from home.

Buchenwald

Down Blutstrasse we might have walked together,
in the permutations of decade and homeland,
a day as crystalline as this, trudging up
from Weimar's depot, listening to wind
in the beech leaves, signing away our rights,
stepping through these green gates one afternoon
when the camp clock still clicked, before liberating
soldiers truncated the time and the hands stopped
forever at 3:15. "Everyone gets what he deserves,"
claims the Gothic script of the gates. I see
a prisoner disinfected and dreaming perhaps
in the blue hills' Thuringian vistas the barracks
ground allows, or aching for the grip
of the voltage-fence, a more exquisite embrace
than any I could give. Caught perhaps
kissing by the Mummelsee or curled naked together
in a Westphalian feather tick, to end here,
amidst these beech woods, this hilltop above the city
where Goethe loved Charlotte as I love you.

A world where your wavy hair is shaved, where
the handsome fur over your chest and belly
fills with lice, where the great muscles
of your arms and shoulders wither with legal famine.
Where hearts are shot full of gasoline,
love is pathology cured with castration,
where starving prisoners watch pet bears
grow fat. Pink triangles: our ashes
might have mixed at last, rich mortar between bricks.

By the line of ovens I stare into ribbed interiors,
a blackness starved, long cold, long cleaned
of ash. Carnations and roses scatter the floor.
How long, at what heat, to roast the body of gay
or Pole or Jew? How long to melt our muscles—

Jeff Mann

this flesh through which delight descends,
moist and laughing, and love is myth no longer—
how long to burn these bodies to ash?

Distant flowers in the breeze,
like a waft of violin. Coexisting, these furnaces,
your face, the gut-throb tenderness I thought long lost.
You are an ocean away, perfectly safe, handsome hubris.
Behind glasses as dark as my beard, through the green gate
I stride free, snapping photos, this pain a curiosity
and luxury, heading towards the air-conditioned tour bus.

The night before liberation, the killing proceeded
in a rush, men like us who once touched gently
and kissed roughly piled cold into carts.
Would love shatter or strengthen in the smell
of such smoke, black disseminations sifting down
among the beeches. How long would hands
grip, stares interlock, before being pulled apart,
all the farewells of history distilled down
into the black points of a man's eyes receding.

3:15 forever. Beech leaves roll over
in the wind, the clovers shiver. Full of tourists,
into 1991 Weimar the bus descends. Some other way
we will separate, some other way we will die,
date and place of birth the only reasons why.

New Market Battlefield

> Would the boys stand, asked Breckinridge. "Yes," replied the major, "they are of the best Virginia blood, and they will."
>
> —*The Battle of New Market*, William C. Davis

A Shenandoah idyll, the Bushong House,
farm turned museum here on the battlefield's edge:
white frame with forest-green shutters
fronting the Blue Ridge castle walls,
rural quaintness I imagine our marriage in.
Separation—six months of autumn and winter—
has melted down like stubborn snow into
the length of this drive, Blacksburg to Boston.
In fantasy, you bend shirtless with high spring
over these daffodils, your trowel meticulous
amidst mulch, the lilac bushes budding like Lazarus.
Where soldiers fell, the orchard froths
with cream beneath the sun's hands,
I wander among apple and cherry blossom,
nuzzling petals like a lover.

In New Market, marriage beds became hospital cots,
parchment-colored sheets ran red,
unstaunched as the Shenandoah whispering
rough about the rocks today, as I stand
on the bluff overlook behind the house.
As Southern as I, these men, too young perhaps
to have felt this fever, this focus that sends me
irrational as budbreak the first week of March
north along the interstates towards you.

The poverty of broomsedge is barren still,
even after all the blood this soil sucked,
this field lined with split-rail and hiss
of dead oak leaves hanging brittle between lives.

From those cloud-clawing silhouettes of oak,
a pair of buzzards lifts, as if carrion were
still heaped, and circles over cannon left like
moraine. The last smudge of morning fog rises
off the river, dews my eyes and beard and ascends,
cloud dissolving into cloud the way bodies would
mingle if they could. Amidst the morgue-pallor
fray of last year's grasses, March sprays green,
soil preparing itself for passion,
new grass thickening like beard or body hair.

They lived long enough to love the South:
the serviceberry's first mist, the forsythia
surging sunny today along the interstate,
grits creamy with long simmer, red eye gravy
with ham on biscuits, the marriage of blossoms
filling these orchards late April and May, pollen
on the eager lips of the wind. Perhaps, with luck,
they learned to love the way good bourbon tastes,
the way, bare beneath a lover, beauty burns like bourbon.
Their graves I cannot find, their names weather elsewhere,
this field where they fell noisy always with truck-roll.

From the same witness oaks a pair of mourning doves
sobs now, and all the bud scales in Appalachia
shudder and soften. I leave New Market Battlefield,
turn onto the interstate north, and the miles
that part us begin to dwindle further.
When after long absence my body slips ecstatic
into yours, our touch will honor these dead,
will give reason to breath. We will honor
the blessed diffusions of muscle into earth,
the dead we will become, the budding our bodies
know together, the orchards that outlive us.

Loving, we know that all who love are kin.

March Magnolias

The saucer magnolias
reconnoiter mid-March,

risking the petal-blackening shrapnel
of last frosts. Every constellation's

rooted in earth, each chalice
of rosé or dilute blood

offered to the clouds' fragmentary whimsy.
Some fire smoulders in our marrows,

the marrow of the earth—
each flower is smoke solidified.

Lifting you into my arms
lifts me. We want to be taken

up. For flowering, to be fuel.
The split rails of chestnut, abandoned

fences burnt, the minerals niched in graves,
dissolved in March rain. Gently

the root hairs poke and stroke and sip,
up xylem the ground water ascends.

This is the rapture they wait for
in all those tiny hillside churches:

like Elijah, we rise
on magnolia blossoms, burning wheels.

With our bodies we enter this heaven
and leave no bones behind.

THREE LOVERS AT WALDEN POND

I have no photo of this: three men stand on the thin beach,
two tied with marriage, two tied with strife and lies.
I do not know why I have come so far,
sixteen hours late winter extends between Blacksburg
and Boston. I do not know whether or how soon
I will end us. Some other layer of psyche
gassed up the pickup and turned the wheel. I only know
one can love a man as Thoreau loved this land,
one can love a rival like a betrayed brother.
To avoid any photo of you two together,
I deliberately forgot the film.
The photographer is always the one absent,
the one who does not belong.

That long-haired and homely misfit I used to be,
pouring over Thoreau in junior high study hall,
how could he know the woodland and solitude
his adolescence ached for would not in adulthood
hold all answers? How could he know how slowly
his loneliness would rot into resignation,
how long it would take for love at last
to be returned, this love he soon must, with fists
and gritted teeth, disbelieving, turn sharply from.
How could he guess how he would at last reach
that pond legendary in the paperback he clutched:
youth all but leached away, woodland all reduced
to mere escape, to diversions of bud scale and leaf fall
beyond ambivalence, arriving this late-winter afternoon
with his lover and his lover's lover, the wilderness
most meaningful now beneath the breastbone.

We stroll first by Concord's shuttered houses.
The quaint subjunctives of marriage: with what fantasy
steamers and chowders I would plump our dark-furred
bellies, what gardens of mints and roses, squash and corn,

you would tend, moist and shirtless, gentle with each fragile
 sprout.
In one field of vision, the churchyard's awful coincidence:
your body, as pure a beauty as earth ever offered,
wrapped this New England March in a long wool coat,
and this leaf-strewn hill of winged-death's-head
dark-slate Yankee headstones, the compost of centuries.

By Walden Pond itself, these chalky groves of white birch
are blank as my body some cryptic karma splits from yours.
The sky and water both film over with the same
satin-gray stratus, cataracts across that fringed eye,
the way long sorrow smudges snowy over sight,
and across the ice, fissure faults cracking clear,
union all illusion, on the edge of tear-melt and drift.
Your shoulders and hips move before me
on the path, your small hand strokes the flank
of oak, silver beginning in your hair
like overcast light in these March-gray coves.

We leave Walden with no photos, only pamphlets.
The next morning and the next, alone together
after all the months apart, we at last make love.
Then I leave our wrestling anarchies of wilderness,
I leave New England down turnpikes edged with snow.
I leave you with a man who has loved you long,
in a life soon healed of me.

Only this certitude remains:
I went to the woods to live deliberately.
I entered the hills of your muscles, the thorn-thickets
of your neuroses, your history, to live deep,
despite risk, despite predetermined loss and lies.
I lifted you onto my sharp need and into my arms,
with fir forests moist on our chests and groins matting
and melding the primal, my hands and mouth and mind
with your flesh, your words, filled and fulfilled.
I sucked sweet what marrow I could, what your fear

and the time-trammelled moment allowed. I left
Walden's winter-empty woods and brittle-iced waters
as certain as Thoreau, holding in memory's metabolism
your beauty as his held these birch-thick hills,
held as proof against any doubt on the deathbed.

Duck Pond In October

Nightfall and I coincide,
scuffing with wind or boot
fallen leaves of weeping willow and oak.

The sparse geese left veer out off violet
in slow angles onto the water,
settle into a satined float, serenity
I cannot comprehend. The mysteries of autumn:
which migrate, which remain.

My beautiful ascensionist, I have avoided
the duck pond for months. A whim turned the wheel
tonight; here I enter again into envy. A few couples
stroll by, avoiding my grief-bristling beard,
my asocial leathers, my glare. There is no danger
in their public touch, no furtive adulteries.
No states sunder their hands.

Why would Adam return after expulsion
to the ruins of Eden? No solace or souvenirs
in ashes. The lover, the wilderness in me
retire. My hands must return
to the uncomplicated warmth of coffee cups,
the shuffle of pages, the refuge
of the steering wheel, the affection of the cat.

> There is nothing left of two men
> who met here in spring. No shimmering
> heat ghosts, no outlines etched
> on air. Two men entranced, knowing
> they would soon, for the first time,
> make love. A frottage of voices,
> the anabolisms of April, the scent of viburnum
> flowers splashing over their shoulders.
> Their shadows coupled and sank into stone.

The water scatters tonight with willow leaves
like ductile tears, the stretch of raindrops
across windshield at interstate speeds.
Scythes bitter gold, as blinding as
the late sun in May splintering off these waters,
tearing my eyes, as I sat stunned, my beard
and hands still scented with you. Hardly enough
experience to recognize happiness.

This loneliness says I have need of ripening yet.
Back to the truck I hurry, cursing myself.
Past the last couples I gear off,

and now the first stars join the drift
of leaves on the water. These are the allotments
of October, a calm catabolism without complaint,
a landscape slowly stripped to its skeleton,
so lucky ever to have had so much to lose.

Bones Washed With Wine

There he was, left behind like silt
or moraine, mineral fragments
in a glass case, Alexander's father,
a curiosity in Thessaloniki. Olympia
had the privilege, after exhumation,
of washing her husband's bones with wine,
nestling them at last in a fine gold box,
with the greaves and delicate oak and acorn
diadems lost to centuries of sunlight.

Last May in Greece, my grief still
forced me forward, not yet a stale
slough. Even losing you made my life
luminous. In Thessaloniki, over café
frappés, over black hissings of surf,
anise-milk ouzo, I imagined our ashes
mixed like the soils of warring countries,
buried in a golden box. Ravenous always,
I devoured baklava, the honey warm
beneath my fangs, calamata olives black
and deliciously bitter as breakage,
and heard our bones rattle like seeds
in a gourd, the embryos of twins
bumping and nestling, accreting like pearls.
I consumed cuttlefish stuffed with feta,
those genital textures, while

    in my mind, in the bed beside you my beard
    filled with silver. Achilles to Patroclus,
    I wrapped your wounds, rubbed red wine
    resin-scented into your chest hair,
    your breastbone, your proud and childish brow,
    dreaming of lasting intimacies, privilege
    certain to be denied. Neither the pulse-
    filled flesh nor the bits of bone after

to grip, own and mourn-bathe with wine.
Some other life, you would say, those second-
chance embodiments you were so sure of,
as you were sure of all else, excusing every action,
every parting impermanent, as if the concept of
other bodies, other bones, other lives could excuse
deprivation, could excuse all injustice now.

Peepers

Between the rushing remote of cars along 460,
this twilit March unravels,

I crane for the wind-chiming peepers.
In the ditch-dregs they sing, bearing

charcoal crosses on tiny backs of green.
The new willows are rilling about them,

and the mourning dove's return,
choking the throat with longing.

Each dusk marks more mileage, an odometer
gauging the distance between our bodies.

You gripped like driftwood the domesticity
you knew, the stagnancy that breeds

wigglers, premature silt-swamps,
clinging less from loyalty than fear.

What landscape cements you now:
the numbered boxes of Reston, broken

glass and crushed samaras in parking lots,
the plaster face of Medusa mounted

on some rented eggshell wall, herbs
coaxed up in tiny root-bound pots.

What passion left to you only lies allow.
All the skin I stroked with frightened

reverence you have long since sloughed off.
Your body was no destination, only

a landscape I travelled through:
the cleavage of low, oak-hairy hills,

the cheek-cupping curves of mossy sandstones,
rock still warm long after sunset.

Land already deeded, of uncertain soil,
else I would gladly have pulled off

the road, along the shaly coltsfoot,
stretched out in the pickup bed,

stretched out along early spring
and twilight and waited, certain

in the silvery song of peepers,
the brusque clack of redwing blackbirds,

those marginal duets rising from
the cattails, certain I had at last

found home, a landscape I would never leave.

Biscuits And Honey

"Famine is unpleasant." —Emily Dickinson

1

This midwinter morning, my Appalachian appetite
immune to the corrosions of despair, bear-like
I break open and butter this biscuit.

A sticky ambush, clover honey.
Years ago, this same chubby plastic bear

> drizzling one spring, one summer
> over your loins, honey lapped

> from the dense night about your nipples.
> Anointing myself, I feed sweetness

> sweetness. I bend to taste myself,
> honey and history upon your parted lips.

> My lips leave droplets, beatitudes,
> upon your drowsing eyelids.

2

Beneath honey, some bodies are bread.
We become gulping angels, all our
appetite become aesthetic. Insatiate,
we lap sweat like liquid gold. We lap
frantic, knowing how soon all honey
dwindles, all sweet and heat
evaporate, how soon the breath-

mist leaves the mirror.
Ravenous as summer, nuzzling
nectar and youth off the flesh,
our tongues strive down
to barriers of bone.

3

With winter, starvation settles in,
new snow swings its scythes across the fields.
Again only the animal can be fed.
With such feasts past, how, with any grace,
any gesture save rage, return to less and less?
Some soul-stuff shrivels.
Grain by grain
the gold reverts,

and I reach for another biscuit.

Confederate Cemetery, Fredericksburg, Virginia

(for Andrea Holland)

In every Southern burying ground
this boxwood smells like fate,
fate that brought these boys down,
in December fog behind the Sunken Road,
boys beneath these tiny markers' uniform
gray, beneath names long rains have half-
effaced. There is more solace here
than many soldiers receive: to dissolve
into the soils of one's homeland, when
the panels of pine not long outlast
the skin. Centuries later men stroll amidst
these stones, praying their easy flesh
might match these bones in honor.

The smell of fate is only timing, sharp-
shooter's aim—the soldier sundered
from his body, my hand releasing yours
on office steps, these maple leaves a skitter
of silver over my boot toes, the wind today
clawing the humped brown grass of graves.

Aimlessness leads me to your surname
in stone. A boy from Covington,
a boy from Powhatan—either in the juggle
of generations could have ended here,
"Mann" and "Taylor" on these Confederate
markers, a convulsive gasp and gripping
in mud behind that battlefield wall,
frosted breath uncurling its last fabrics
along such a wind as this. Above the Taylor
tombstone the hollies bleed and bead—

so agony must bubble up about the bullet
and embers shudder on amidst ashen devour.
How often love outlasts even hope.

For me, in Southern soil the plot
is already allotted. For another,
where will that body loved and begged
and clutched like breath, those muscles
and bones unknit? Such parting is practice—
so we lose our lovers' bodies and learn
with more grace to lose our own. Brother,
may Virginian earth hold you close and safe
as I once could. This holly berry I pluck
and hold over your tomb pulses
in my palm as your heart once did.
This burning seed, before I give it back
to you—before my voice sinks silent,
as wind dies down with nightfall
into brown and sutured sod—
brother, give me your last breath.

Scotch And Valentines

Sentimental over Scotch, I request "My Funny Valentine"
in the second set. She rolls it out like velvet
in a fabric store, the textures of rabbit's belly
or horse's chin. I lift my glass in salute,
watch light suspend in Glenfiddich's golden volatiles,

                    and now
    I am leaning over you again, propping one arm
    against the greenhouse door, whispering
    "You're my favorite work of art."
    Midsummer, passionflowers whirl along
    the trellis, high wind shivers the plumes
    of pampas grass. Inside, the potato plants
    you've tended scrabble towards light, a prisoner
    shaking bars, a premature burial. We still believe
    gentle germinations are possible between us,
    pure phototropism is urging us together.
    Beneath your T-shirt my hands are all reverence,
    the awe of the connoisseur, as if Praxiteles spoke
    the prayers of Pygmalion. Flawless Olympic marble
    pulses warm beneath my stroke, dark grass grows wet
    with rain. Our alchemy rescues flesh from stone.

This winter I am stone again, amazed nevertheless
at how songs exhume. After every dreaded
ending, first a vague nostalgia. Then
the rage of the robbed, stomach full of pumice
chunks, sick to heal, to forget. Finally,
one night sipping single malt straight, wind
hissing around the bar like snow snaking
high-speed off a carhood, this night I know
how few intoxicants seize the soul. Tonight,
suddenly, I want to remember, I want to whisper
along "My Funny Valentine," remember that face
and voice and body, that eau de vie nakedness

that made kindling of me down to bone, when
no cell was stone or sober. Any proof
that bliss exists, as we stroke the silver
swollen buds of star magnolia, know all
the cynical hazards of late frost, but
anticipate nevertheless. As farmers all winter
by their hearths sort and order seeds,
as leaf scars along the twigs of oak reveal
not only loss but proof the earth shifts
its weight day by day towards birth again
when another generation will touch.

Another Droning Dismissal

Late winter, the moan of mourning
doves again. This year let yearning
enter other lives.

On the balcony, disappearing,
the greeting a guest cut
into crusted snow.

A wrist I gripped until
it bruised. I was determined
my touch would leave some trace.

The first warm weekend, the lovers
stroll arm in arm, hand in hand,
the way rails at night converge

their silver, a creek slips mud
into the Greenbrier River's stream.
The lovers sip cokes, order ice creams,

they party late, disturb my sleep.
When the chill rains return, I am
grateful. May it remain winter forever,

may the reservoir always be iced over,
the sycamores flake off superfluous
skin. I have no deeper words

for you than this hasty
legal-pad scrawl, this litany
of professional successes.

Snow is an excuse to remain within,
to drink Irish whiskey or kirsch.
How deftly we have learned to control

these interiors. Even my dreams
can barely remember the curves
of your arms or your brow or your chest.

A wet mist swallows the mountains.
My prayers keep it low. It will not
lift. Less present, the absent,

the first acrid smoke off campfires
just doused. To what we find most
beautiful, to what we cannot possess, we speak

again and again, casually (parenthetical
dismissal), as if conversation could
make anything easier to part with,

could make mundane the miraculous.

Not Getting Off At Farragut North

Something sickeningly mathematical in this,
he thinks. Lines perpendicular, crossing
but on different planes. Like flying over
a city left in tears long ago, craning against
the smudgy Lufthansa porthole, sailing with
cirrus over Boston, knowing down there
lives someone still loved, knowing altitude
makes us all microscopic eventually.

Today he does not get off at Farragut North.
He will visit no one today. He will buy
aquavit and raclette cheese, he will buy
and begin the Alexandria Quartet, enjoying
those purchased urban pleasures his small
hometown cannot provide. He will not
leave his seat at this stop, ride the escalator
like some rainbow bridge. He will not
step into the sun, squinting like some ghoul,
look for L Street, step into the bookstore,
ask for the manager. Some meetings are moot.
They lead to nothing, like rails that run
into a collapsed tunnel, off a broken bridge,
a tripped drunk's brow bloodied with
the kiss of brick. Now the "bee-bum"

bird call; on that chance, the doors
nip together like knives. With the niched
concrete of the Metro stop, the subjunctive
rushes past, as details are mercifully
smeared by speed. Against that racing black
his reflection shoulders steady: dark
glasses, dark beard, silver earring, black
leather jacket and cap. A study
in grim defense, a skin of obsidian,

the black crust into which the molten stiffen.
No one can love so much shadow.
The couple necking before him he wants
to strike. In the black snow-grit

of volcanic fallout swallowing the olive
groves, the grape arbors, one man dies
curled about another, stone niched forever
in stone. Now all the world is ash.

At a safer stop, the shadow on the train
rises. Fascinated by his own reflection,
he forgets his book. On the platform,
he turns. Awareness is a cursing.
Too late, lover. Unread, it disappears
between the blinking blue lights
that mark the tunnel's entrance and end.

Leaf Stains

They want to be remembered,
these maple leaves sticking
to a sidewalk after rain.

Even after wind ushers them off,
the pressing fervor of their palms
leaves a tannic stain—the richness

of rivers rising on a flood plain,
lakes glistening in the glacier's wake,
the web dawn-spiders trail

across dewberry vines, the fading
scars a comet carves across indigo.
So the cave-dwellers once dipped

their palms in paint and pressed them
against the deepest chambers' walls.
Years ago, beneath your ardor,

a few bruises once bloomed
along my inner thigh, dark clouds
that paled day by day into history.

Miraculous, for touch to mean so much,
yet to leave temporary marks or none.
I stripped in the late winter light,

offered up my body as if you were
priest or king, as if your hands
could heal. I grasped you roughly,

wanting to be remembered. To brand
the scrimshaw of my signature
along your sternum, along your spine.

Not to end this petty surface stain,
a hard grip's red trace
evaporating from pale skin,

the leaves' brown epitaph
the rains evoke
and the rains erase.

Books Available from Gival Press

Barnyard Buddies I by Pamela Brown; illustrations by Annie H. Hutchins
1st edition, ISBN 1-928589-15-4, $16.00

Thirteen stories filled with a cast of creative creatures both engaging and educational. "These stories in this series are delightful. They are wise little fables, and I found them fabulous." — Robert Morgan, author of *This Rock* and *Gap Creek*

Bones Washed With Wine: Flint Shards from Sussex and Bliss by Jeff Mann
1st edition, ISBN 1-928589-14-6, $15.00

A special collection of lyric intensity, including the 1999 Gival Press Poetry Award winning collection. Jeff Mann is "a poet to treasure both for the wealth of his language and the generosity of his spirit." — Edward Falco, author of *Acid*

Canciones para sola cuerda — Songs for a Single String by Jesús Gardea
English translation by Robert L. Giron 1st edition, ISBN 1-928589-09-X, $15.00

A moving collection of love poems, with echoes of Neruda à la Mexicana. "Jesús Gardea's poetry awakens a distant, almost forgotten primeval yearning that compels us to find that elusive woman whom we have met only in our dreams, but whose presence we sense will complete us."
— Carlos Rubio Albet, author of *The Neophyte: A Dubious Beginning*

Dervish by Gerard Wozek
1st edition, ISBN 1-928589-11-1, $15.00

Winner of the 2000 Gival Press Poetry Award. This rich whirl of the dervish traverses a grand expanse from bars to crazy dreams to fruition of desire. "By Jove, these poems shimmer." — Gerry Gomez Pearlberg, author of *Mr. Bluebird*

Dreams and Other Ailments — Sueños y otros achaques by Teresa Bevin
1st edition, ISBN 1-928589-13-8, $21.00

Winner of the Bronze Award - 2001 ForeWord Magazine's Book of the Year Award for Translation. A wonderful array of short stories about the fantasy of life and tragedy but filled with humor and hope. "*Dreams and Other Ailments* will lift your spirits." — Dr. Lynne Greeley, Professor of Theatre, University of Vermont

The Gay Herman Melville Reader by Ken Schellenberg
    1ˢᵗ edition, ISBN 1-928589-19-7, $16.00

> A superb selection of Melville's work. "Here in one anthology are the selections from which a serious argument can be made by both readers and scholars that a subtext exists that can be seen as homoerotic."
> — David Garrett Izzo, author of *Christopher Isherwood: His Era, His Gang, and the Legacy of the Truly Strong Man*

Let Orpheus Take Your Hand by George Klawitter
    1ˢᵗ edition, ISBN 1-928589-16-2, $15.00

> *Winner of the 2001 Gival Press Poetry Award*. A thought provoking work that mixes the spiritual with stealthy desire, with Orpheus leading us out of the pit. "These poems present deliciously sly metaphors of the erotic life that keep one reading on, and chuckling with pleasure." — Edward Field, author of *Stand Up, Friend, With Me*

Metamorphosis of the Serpent God by Robert L. Giron
    1ˢᵗ ed., ISBN 1-928589-07-3, $12.00

> "Robert Giron's biographical poetry embraces the past and the present, ethnic and sexual identity, themes both mythical and personal."
> — The Midwest Book Review

The Nature Sonnets by Jill Williams
    1ˢᵗ edition, ISBN 1-928589-10-3, $8.95

> An innovative collection of sonnets that speaks to the cycle of nature and life, crafted with wit and clarity. "Refreshing and pleasing."
> — Miles David Moore, author of *The Bears of Paris*

Songs for the Spirit by Robert L. Giron
    1ˢᵗ ed., ISBN 1-928589-08-1, $16.95

> This humanist psalter reflects a vision of the new millennium, one that speaks to readers regardless of their religion. "This is an extraordinary book." — John Shelby Spong, author of *Why Christianity Must Change or Die: A Bishop Speaks to Believers in Exile*

Wrestling with Wood by Robert L. Giron
    3ʳᵈ ed., ISBN 1-928589-05-7, $5.95

> A chapbook of impressionist moods and feelings of a long-term relationship which ended in a tragic death. "Nuggets of truth and beauty sprout within our souls." — Teresa Bevin, author of *Havana Split*

For Book Orders Only, Call: 800.247.6553
Or Write : Gival Press, LLC / PO Box 3812 / Arlington, VA 22203
Or Visit: www.givalpress.com

www.ingramcontent.com/pod-product-compliance
Lightning Source LLC
Chambersburg PA
CBHW031209090426
42736CB00009B/853